Catastrophe!

Great Engineering Failure—and Success

Scientific American Mysteries of Science

Catastrophe!

Great Engineering Failure—and Success

by Fred Bortz

illustrations by Gary Tong

Scientific American

BOOKS FOR YOUNG READERS

W. H. Freeman and Company / New York

In memory of my father,

Harry A. Bortz (1901-1991),

who taught me not to fear failure, nor to accept it,

but to learn from it in order to succeed.

Acknowledgments

Thanks to those Carnegie Mellon University colleagues who replied to my electronic bulletin board request for "favorite catastrophes," especially Robert Frederking, who sent me looking for Flight 401; Roni Rosenfeld, who reminded me of the Great Northeast Blackout; and Randy Brost, who reminded me of the original Murphy's Law story.
Much of the information in Chapter 2 is drawn from the writings of Professor Henry Petroski of Duke University, whose book *To Engineer Is Human: The Role of Failure in Successful Design* you might enjoy reading when you are a bit older. The idea to write *Catastrophe!* arose after the author attended a lecture by Professor Petroski on the topic of that book at Carnegie Mellon University's Engineering Design Research Center.

—F. B.

Thanks to Bill Kapp, engineer and pilot, and Mike Cook, flight simulator and instructor, for their professional assistance with information on airplanes and aviation.

—G. T.

Text copyright © 1995 Alfred B. Bortz.
Illustrations copyright © 1995 W. H. Freeman and Company. All rights reserved.

Scientific American Books for Young Readers is an imprint of
W. H. Freeman and Company, 41 Madison Avenue, New York, NY 10010.

Book design by Richard Oriolo

Library of Congress Cataloging-in-Publication Data

Bortz, Alfred B.
Catastrophe! : great engineering failure—and success / by Fred Bortz.
Includes index.
ISBN 0-7167-6538-1. — ISBN 0-7167-6539-X (pbk.)
1. Engineering—Juvenile literature. 2. System failures (Engineering)—
Juvenile literature. [1. Engineering. 2. Disasters. 3. Accidents.] I. Title.
TA149.B67   1995   620-dc20   94-37774   CIP   AC

Printed in the United States of America.

10 9 8 7 6 5 4 3 2 1

Contents

Obeying Murphy's Law

When you are in a hurry and all the traffic lights are red . . . when soup spills on your best clothes . . . when your pencil point breaks in the middle of a test . . . that's what most people call Murphy's Law: "Whatever can go wrong will go wrong."

In 1948, Captain Edward A. Murphy was the best trouble-shooting engineer on the United States Air Force's Rocket Sled project led by Major John Paul Stapp. Stapp, a physician and test pilot, wanted to know how the human body responds to high acceleration—rapid changes in speed and direction. Stapp's project was important because scientists and engineers were developing jet planes that could change speed and direction faster than ever before, and they were beginning to think about sending people on rockets into space.

The Rocket Sled could accelerate very rapidly, reaching speeds up to 632 miles per hour (about 275 meters per second) in only five seconds. It could stop even faster, some-

times going from top speed to a full stop in as little as 1.4 seconds. A person riding on the sled would feel enormous forces, which scientists determined by measuring the acceleration or deceleration in comparison to the acceleration of Earth's gravity. The safety harness of a passenger experiencing a deceleration of 30 G's would restrain him with a force 30 times his weight.

Stapp didn't want to risk the life or health of any of his team members, so he rode the sled himself. Every trip was a wild ride. When the sled accelerated, he felt as if an elephant was standing on his chest while someone peeled the skin from his face. Then, when the brakes were applied, he felt like he was being slammed into a brick wall.

One day, Stapp climbed into the sled and was strapped into his seat for a ride faster than 31 G's. When he got out, he asked how fast he had gone this time. Each of the sled's six G-meters read zero!

Stapp asked Captain Murphy to find out what had gone wrong. Murphy discovered the problem: The G-meters had been installed backward. Recalling the incident in 1983 for an article in *People* magazine, Murphy said he had told Stapp, "If there's more than one way

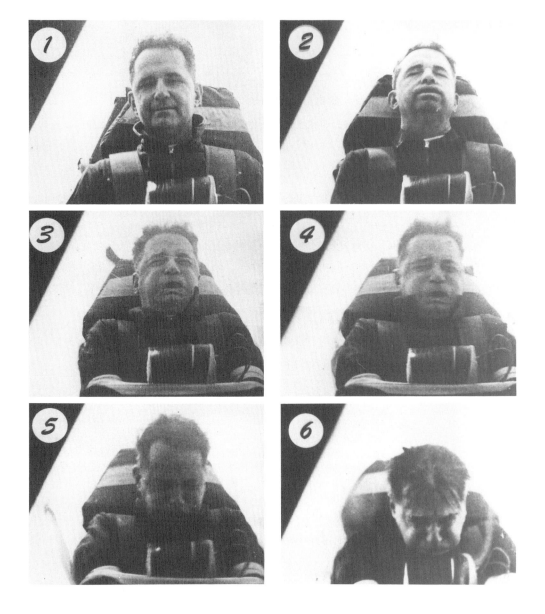

to do a job and one of them will end in disaster, then somebody will do it that way." He remembers Stapp's reply as, "That is Murphy's Law."

A few weeks after being victimized by the backward G-meters incident, Stapp gave an Air Force press conference a different version: "If something can go wrong, it will." The reporters loved it. From that day until now, "Murphy's Law" has been part of our language—although incorrectly stated.

What Captain Murphy really meant was that engineers should always be careful to look for anything that can lead to failure in their designs—and eliminate it.

Of course, engineers are human, so they sometimes miss something that can go wrong. When they do, according to Murphy's Law, failure will certainly follow. If they are good engineers like Murphy, they learn from that failure, whether it is big or small.

In fact, they learn far more from failure than from success, including the failures of others. For example, the Rocket Sled experience told them to design parts that can be installed in only one way, so if someone tries to put them in backward or upside down, they don't fit.

Because people don't like to talk about what they did wrong, most small failures are never reported. That's too bad, because small failures can teach us how to avoid larger ones. But when catastrophes occur—sudden, unexpected, or tragic failures—they attract attention. People talk about them, study them, and—we hope—learn from them.

In this book you'll read about spectacular engineering failures, some of which were tragic and catastrophic. More importantly, you'll discover that spectacular success is possible when you truly understand the causes of failure.

That's what Murphy's Law really means: *If you want things to go right, pay attention to everything that can go wrong*. Now that's a law worth obeying!

Chapter 1

Dance of Death

I n July 1980, people gasped in wonder as they entered the spectacular lobby of the newly opened Kansas City, Missouri Hyatt Regency Hotel. A year later, they gasped in horror.

Like many hotels built at that time, the 40-story Kansas City Hyatt featured a huge, bright open area called an atrium at its center. Visitors looking upward from the ground floor lobby had a dramatic view. Three walkways, each 10 feet (3 meters) wide and 75 feet (230 meters) long, called sky bridges or skywalks, hung gracefully from the ceiling of the atrium, connecting the meeting rooms on one side of the second, third, and fourth floors to the sleeping rooms on the other. Everyone loved the skywalks. People would cross them simply for the sensation of walking on air. On Friday nights, people flocked to the new Hyatt for the weekly Tea Dance. They looked forward to an evening of dancing, socializing, and enjoying their favorite foods while listening to Big Band sounds. Many people loved danc-

4th-floor walkway

Function block

West side of atrium

3rd-floor walkway

2nd-floor walkway

Kansas City Hyatt original lobby

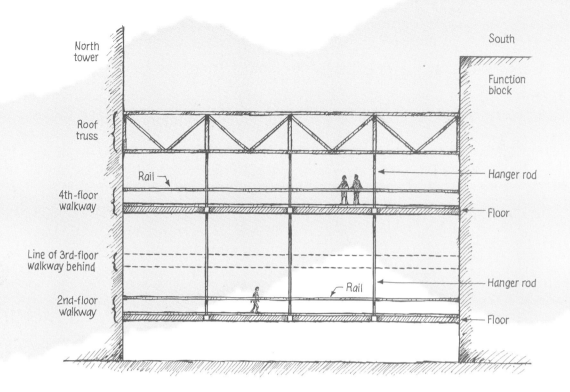

ing on the skywalks, which seemed to sway gently with them as the music echoed from the lobby below.

The Tea Dance became so popular that at 7:00 P.M. on Friday, July 17, 1981, about 1,500 people were in the Hyatt lobby or on the skywalks. Suddenly and without warning, the fourth-floor walkway collapsed. Along with the second-floor walkway, directly underneath, it came crashing down to the lobby floor. The tragic accident left 114 people dead and about 200 injured.

In the days immediately following the accident, the newspapers were full of questions. What caused the collapse? Were too many people on the walkways? Did their dancing put too much strain on the steel support rods? Was there a weak spot in a rod or in a connector between a rod and the walkway? Who was at fault?

It took months of investigation and analysis to come up with the answers. Most of the analysis was done by engineers. Why? Because engineers spend most of their career dealing with failure.

Now, if you know any engineers, that statement may seem odd to you. Ask them what they do, and they'll tell you about their successes, not their failures. They'll talk about how they create machines, structures, or devices—cars or bridges or computer chips or other

technological wonders. They will describe how they design and build their creations to function as we, the users, have come to expect. They often call their creations *artifacts* because they are created artificially rather than naturally.

Of the engineering artifacts all around us, most work in the way they were intended to. Their creators have spent hours thinking about what might cause failure and then working out ways to prevent it.

But thinking about failure isn't enough. Engineers must also test their artifacts, looking for the smallest signs of trouble and correcting the problems they find. Finally, they study the artifacts in use. Again they pay attention to problems and failures, large and small, and again they change the artifacts to make them work more successfully.

Despite all these precautions, engineered artifacts sometimes fail. Sometimes, as in the case of the Kansas City Hyatt skywalks, the failure is catastrophic. That means it happens suddenly, unpredictably, and has serious consequences for the artifact and for objects and living things nearby.

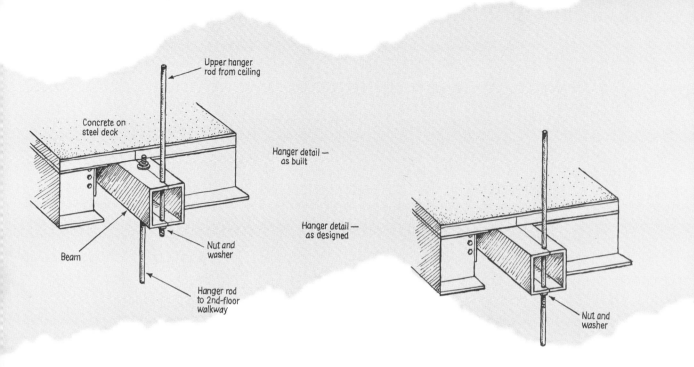

The only good thing about a catastrophic failure is that people cannot fail to notice it and therefore can learn valuable lessons from it.

How Could It Happen?

High above the twisted metal in the hotel lobby, a team of accident investigators studied the steel rods that had once supported the fallen walkways. The rods had hung down from the ceiling and passed through small holes in the walkway. Large nuts had fastened the walkway to the rods. Although the walkway was now on the floor, the nuts were still firmly attached to the rods. Was the downward force on the walkway great enough to stretch the holes until the nuts passed through, the investigators wondered.

Next they examined the holes in the walkway where the rods had been connected. They discovered that the holes *had* become large enough for the nuts to pass through. When one nut passed through its hole, the force on the metal around the other rods became unbearable. The walkways fell.

Checking the original engineering drawings, investigators were puzzled. The support should not have failed. It was designed to be strong enough to hold more than twice the weight of the walkway. Even the downward force of people standing shoulder to shoulder and dancing to the music shouldn't have enlarged the holes.

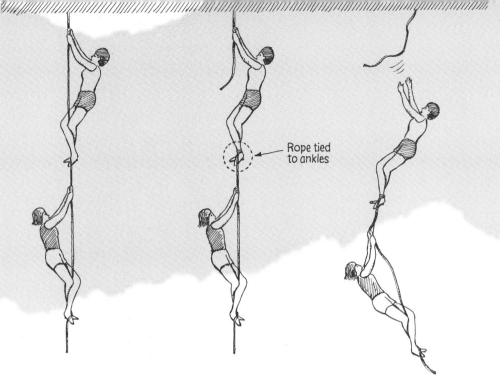

Rope tied to ankles

But the walkways had not followed their original design. The second- and fourth-floor walkways were supposed to have been attached to the same rod, with nuts to hold them in place. Building it that way was another matter. It was too hard for the builder to cut screw threads and attach large nuts partway down the long support rods. So the builder suggested a design change.

As you can see in the drawing, the change seemed innocent: Simply replace each long rod with two shorter ones. In the changed design, the fourth-floor walkway hangs from the top of the atrium on one set of short rods, and the second-floor walkway hangs from the fourth-floor walkway on the other set.

But the change was not innocent. You can understand how it led to tragedy by thinking of the support rods as ropes hanging from the ceiling and the walkways as gymnasts hanging from the ropes.

In the original design, two gymnasts are hanging onto the same rope. The rope is strong enough to hold both of them, and each of them is strong enough to support her own weight.

In the changed design, one gymnast hangs onto the rope. A second rope is tied around her ankles, and another gymnast hangs onto that one. The ropes are strong enough, as before, and the lower gymnast can hang on just fine. The top one, however, suddenly has to support not only her own weight but the weight of the other as well. She hangs on for a while, until gradually her grip weakens. Suddenly, she lets go, and both gymnasts fall together.

In a similar way, the upper supports had to carry the weight of the two skywalks, which was nearly as much as they could withstand. The added weight of the people, plus the extra stress caused by their motion, led to the catastrophic failure of the upper supports and the collapse of the two skywalks.

The lessons from Kansas City are as useful to an ordinary person as they are to an engineer. One lesson is this: *A simple idea is not always simple to carry out.* In this case, the simple design required the builder to find a way to cut threads and attach a nut in the middle of a very long rod. That proved to be so difficult that it led to a design change.

Another lesson is: A *small change may have large and unexpected consequences.* At first glance, replacing a long rod with two shorter ones appeared to affect only the connection holding up the second-floor walkway. But in fact, it more than doubled the force between the nut and the metal of the fourth-floor walkway.

A third lesson is: *Success depends on paying attention to detail.* Many people were involved in making and approving the design change. Because it looked simple, they overlooked the details.

The Kansas City Hyatt tragedy illustrates one of engineering's most important sayings: "Experience tests first and teaches later." You learn how to do things better from the problems you encounter along the way.

Does that mean that the tragedy was unavoidable, that successful skywalks could be built only after the experience of a collapse? Of course not. The engineering lessons of the skywalk failure had been taught many times before. Unfortunately, it took a tragedy for some people to learn them.

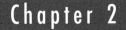

Chapter 2

Gertie's Last Gallop

On the morning of November 7, 1940, the weather report for the Tacoma, Washington, area called for winds a bit higher than usual. Everyone knew what that meant: "Galloping Gertie," the recently completed bridge spanning the Tacoma Narrows, would be treating those who drove across it to a roller-coaster ride.

On calm days, the roadway of the new Tacoma Narrows Bridge was flat and steady. The half-mile ride above the narrow waterway at the southern tip of Puget Sound was smooth. But when the wind kicked up, the bridge deck resembled the waves on the water below, rising and falling gently and rhythmically. Its peaks were so high and its valleys so deep that drivers would see the cars ahead disappearing and reappearing as they rose and fell.

For some drivers and passengers, it was an adventure. For others, it spelled danger, and they went miles out of their way to avoid it.

WASHINGTON

Bremerton
Seattle
Tacoma

Area of detail

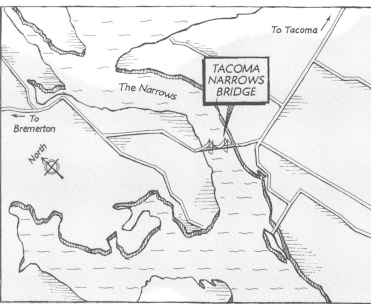

To Tacoma

TACOMA
NARROWS
BRIDGE

The Narrows

To
Bremerton

North

Problems with the bridge had first come up during construction. Several workers had actually become seasick from the up-and-down movement. But engineers who studied the bridge, such as Professor Burt Farquharson of the University of Washington, said that people could use it safely. Meanwhile, he and other experts worked on design changes that would reduce the bridge's sensitivity to wind currents.

The situation changed suddenly that November morning. The bridge's motion loosened a band that held one of its supporting cables in place, and the roadway began to twist from side to side. Drivers struggled to keep their cars from being tossed into the other lane, and the bridge was closed to traffic.

Professor Farquharson saw it all. He had gone to the Narrows to observe the bridge and to compare its motion with that of a model in his laboratory. When the twisting began, he rushed to a camera shop to borrow motion picture equipment. He quickly set up the camera.

One of the most memorable scenes in the Farquharson film shows the professor walking unsteadily toward the single remaining car on the roadway. The car's driver, a reporter, had abandoned it after it stalled and slid into the wrong lane. He had clung to the curb and finally, during a pause in the bridge's motion, was able to crawl to safety with the news story of his life. But he had to leave behind his small dog, trapped inside the car.

Professor Farquharson, noting that the bridge's center line was nearly steady as the bridge deck twisted about it, set out to save the animal. Before he could reach the car, however, the motion increased to the danger level. The professor turned back and got off the bridge just in time to witness Gertie's final, catastrophic gallop: a violent twisting that tore the bridge apart. The dog was the only creature lost, and Professor Farquharson became the star of his own unplanned movie classic.

With all the bridges that people had built before 1940, you would think that the designers of the Tacoma Narrows Bridge could have created it to withstand the breezes of a Washington autumn. In fact, soon after Gertie's final gallop, they did exactly that. The redesigned Tacoma Narrows Bridge has carried traffic safely and steadily between Tacoma and the Olympic Peninsula since then.

So what went wrong the first time?

Bridges and the Human Imagination

The designers of Galloping Gertie wanted to make their bridge as spectacular as the narrows it spanned. They hoped it would become a tribute to human ingenuity and imagination.

The designers knew that to bridge a gap as wide and deep as the Tacoma Narrows, they would have to build a suspension bridge, a roadway suspended—hung—from two huge towers by massive steel cables. Imposing towers and gracefully curving cables would make the bridge a work of art as well as one of engineering.

In 1937, three years before Gertie began to gallop, another graceful West Coast suspension bridge—San Francisco's Golden Gate—had captured the American imagination. Gertie's designers no doubt learned many lessons from the success of the Golden Gate. Unfortunately, they missed some lessons from New York City's Bronx-Whitestone bridge, which had opened to traffic in 1939. Those lessons became clear only after Gertie collapsed.

The roadways of both the Bronx-Whitestone and Tacoma Narrows bridges were laid on solid steel girders about 8 feet (2.4 meters) deep. That was a change in design from bridges like the Golden Gate, which supported their roadways on 20 to 30 feet (6 to 9 meters) high boxlike open trusses of steel bars, connected much like a toy Erector set. The new design saved money and created a more graceful appearance. In comparison to the giant bridge towers, the 8-foot (2.4-meter) roadway structures looked like narrow ribbons floating in air.

When the six-lane Bronx-Whitestone Bridge was completed, its roadway, much to the engineers' surprise, danced in the wind. They immediately added extra cables and stiffening devices, which kept the motion down to only a few inches. It was safe, but the up-and-down motion made many travelers between the Bronx (on the New York mainland) and Long Island feel uneasy.

The motion should have been a hint to the builders of the two-lane Tacoma Narrows Bridge that design changes were needed. Had they fully understood it, they would have stopped construction. But they didn't realize that the relatively small problem on the Bronx-Whitestone project would be catastrophic for their much narrower and somewhat longer roadway.

What was the problem? Engineers who designed bridges at that time decided not to include aerodynamic forces in their calculations. It wasn't that they didn't know aerodynamics, the science that describes the effects that moving gases and liquids have on objects in their paths. They used its complicated mathematical formulas in designing airplanes and

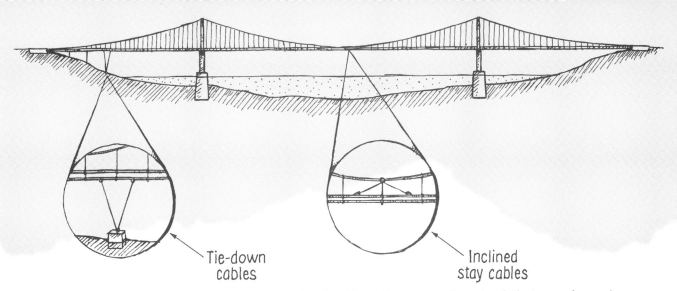

Tie-down cables

Inclined stay cables

streamlined cars. But until Gertie's final gallop, they never imagined that aerodynamic forces on a bridge could be so great. They didn't realize that the graceful long and narrow deck of their bridge would behave a bit like an airplane wing.

After Gertie

Since that windy November day in Tacoma, bridge design has never been the same. No one would think of designing a suspension bridge without doing a full aerodynamic analysis. And no one would think of building one without first testing a laboratory model.

As you might imagine, one of the first tasks after Gertie's collapse was to stiffen the Bronx-Whitestone Bridge. Even so, it remained sensitive to the wind. As late as the 1980s, engineers were still making improvements to reduce its motion.

Before Gertie

Long before engineering existed, people looked for ways to make bridges to shorten or ease their way across streams and valleys. They learned by trial and error. When they found a method to bridge one stream, they applied that to a slightly more difficult crossing. Of course, any method has its limits. When people pushed a method a little too far, their bridge would fail.

Failure didn't stop their progress. They would just try something else. Over time, people learned to use scientific observations and mathematical formulas to decide what to try next. Bridge builders became engineers. Did that mean that trial-and-error learning was past? Not at all! The trials became more ambitious and the errors became more spectacular. From time to time, a grand bridge project would end in catastrophic failure.

Each bridge failure had lessons to teach. Sometimes they learned those lessons. Sometimes they didn't know enough to recognize them. Sometimes—inexcusably—they ignored them.

Most experts would place the collapse of Galloping Gertie in the middle category. The problems of the Bronx-Whitestone Bridge could have drawn the Tacoma Narrows Bridge designers' attention to aerodynamics, but no one saw the connection. Had they known the details of the collapse of the five-year-old Wheeling Suspension Bridge across the Ohio River on May 17, 1854, they might have recognized the problem. But their training was based on engineering books and journals, not on old newspaper articles like this one in the Wheeling *Intelligencer*, which could well have been describing Professor Farquharson's experience with Galloping Gertie.

> About 3 o'clock yesterday we walked toward the Suspension Bridge and went upon it, as we have frequently done, enjoying the cool breeze and the undulating motion of the bridge. . . . We had been off the flooring [deck] only two minutes and were on Main Street when we saw persons running toward the river bank; we followed just in time to see the whole structure heaving and dashing with tremendous force.
>
> For a few moments, we watched it with breathless anxiety, lunging like a ship in a storm; at one time it rose to nearly the height of the tower. . . . At last there seemed to be a determined twist along the entire span, about one half of the floor-ing being nearly reversed, and down went the immense structure from its dizzy height to the stream below, with an appalling crash and roar.

The Greatness of the Golden Gate

Sometimes a bridge's true greatness is revealed in an unplanned way. In 1987, San Franciscans celebrated the 50th anniversary of the Golden Gate Bridge with a bridge walk. On its opening in 1937, a similar event drew 200,000 people over the course of a day. This time more than 750,000 people showed up, and as many as 250,000 of them were packed onto the bridge at one time.

The roadway, which normally takes the form of an arch at the middle of the bridge, flattened, and the bridge began to sway in forty-mile-per-hour winds. Engineers calculated that the bridge was more heavily loaded by that event than at any time in its history. Imagine the tragedy that would have resulted from a catastrophic failure due to that unex-pected load.

Unhappy Landings

Since ancient times, people have dreamed of flying. In an ancient Greek legend, a man named Daedalus fashions huge wax-and-feather wings so he and his son, Icarus, can escape from a maze on an island in the sea. Daedalus warns Icarus not to fly too high, where the sun's rays would melt the wax, nor too low, where the salt spray from the sea would ruin the feathers.

Unfortunately, Icarus is so thrilled by flying that he forgets his father's words. He soars upward until the wax melts. The carefully engineered wings fail catastrophically, and he falls to his death.

British author Stephen Barlay, in *Aircraft Detective,* a serious book about the investigation of airplane crashes, has a different and amusing explanation for what must have happened to Icarus. The wax would not have melted, because Icarus would not have been much closer to the sun. Instead, he would have flown through some very chilly air, which would have made the wax hard and brittle. When Icarus flapped with great strength to climb higher, the wax would have cracked and the wings fallen apart.

You may think it is silly to argue about an ancient myth. But Barlay makes an important point: To prevent harm to future fliers, it is important to understand the causes of past aircraft failures.

Are Airplanes Safe?

In many countries of the world, air travel has become a routine part of life. Modern airplanes carry hundreds of people at more than 600 miles (1,000 kilometers) per hour. Planes sometimes crash, killing most or all on board. So why do people fly?

The answer is that flying is safer than many other activities of everyday life. People are killed or injured riding in cars or buses, crossing the street, playing a favorite sport, or falling at home! Nearly everything you do carries some small risk of death or injury, but most people live long lives with few injuries and die of natural causes.

People who fly put their trust in the people who designed and built the planes, the crews who pilot them, the people who predict and watch for dangerous weather, and the air-traffic controllers who guide them to safe take-off and landing.

Air travel is safe largely because people have always recognized its dangers. When there is a crash, investigators try to understand what happened so they can prevent it from happening again. Planes carry cockpit voice recorders and instruments known as flight recorders. These preserve information about the crew and the plane's most important mechanical and electrical parts, from takeoff right up to the crash.

Countries all over the world have laws to ensure safe travel. There are also national and international bodies, like the National Transportation Safety Board in the United States, that study every plane crash and many near-accidents to see what they can learn .

"I Fall to Pieces"

No one expects an airplane to fall apart or explode during a flight, but sometimes it happens. Fliers may fall helplessly to their deaths, but unlike Icarus, they usually do not disappear forever beneath the waves while pieces of their aircraft scatter in the wind. Rather, investigators recover as much of the aircraft as possible and study every piece for clues to what went wrong. Sometimes the voice and flight recorders tell the tale, but usually the full

"Black box"

DC-10

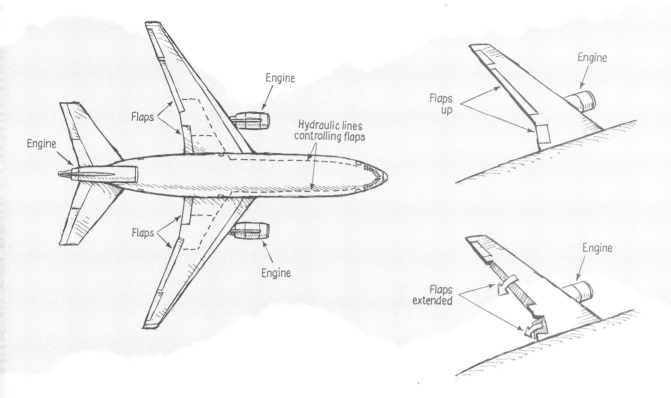

story is found only in the many pieces of wreckage strewn over the crash scene.

Sometimes a new-model plane has flaws that go undetected until after a crash. Even then, investigators may have trouble pinpointing the problem, especially when crash damage is severe. Tragically, there may be several crashes before someone sees a pattern of failure. That was the case with a type of airplane called a DC-10 in the late 1970s and early 1980s.

On May 25, 1979, an American Airlines DC-10 was taking off from Chicago's O'Hare International Airport, when one of its three engines tore off the wing. As dangerous as this was, the plane was designed so it could fly even in that condition. But as the engine and its support ripped away, the cables controlling the flaps on that wing were cut.

The flaps are extended to give the plane the extra aerodynamic lift it needs to take off quickly. Without the cables, the flaps on the DC-10's damaged wing pulled back. The lift on the wings became dangerously unbalanced.

Even so, the pilot could still have brought the plane under control if he had known what the problem was. Unfortunately, more than the flap cables were cut as the engine tore away. Also cut were four hoses that carried a fluid to control two warning signals. Either one of those warnings would have told the pilot that the flaps on the damaged wing had retracted.

Paris shortly after its takeoff on March 3, 1974, killing 346. Since bombs on planes were a serious problem at that time, terrorist involvement was suspected. Six bodies and bits of the plane were scattered over a large area around the crash site, but the plane's cargo door was found far away from the rest of the pieces.

Crash investigators concluded that the cargo door had not been properly locked and had blown open, leading to the crash. An improved cargo door design eliminated the possibility of improper locking in the future.

As you might imagine, many people avoided flying on DC-10s for some time following the O'Hare crash and the Dulles and Miami incidents. Passengers, understandably, remained uneasy about the aircraft for a while following the 1982 design change. But as this book is being written, passengers once again board DC-10s, confident of happy landings ahead.

"I Never Saw It Coming"

What could be more catastrophic—sudden and unpredictable—than a plane flying steadily and smoothly into an unseen swamp or mountain? Airplane crashes of this type, called CFIT (Controlled Flight Into Terrain) accidents, seldom occur. They usually indicate that something caused the crew to be unaware of danger.

One of the most famous CFIT accidents occurred just before midnight on December 29, 1972. Eastern Airlines Flight 401, a Lockheed L-1011 wide-body aircraft, was approaching Miami after a flight from New York with 176 people on board. As the crew prepared the plane for landing, they noticed a problem. Normally, a light would turn on to indicate that the landing gear was safely down and locked. This time, the light was off.

One of the most likely causes of a missing indicator light is a burned-out bulb, but flight crews are trained not to take chances. The pilot notified the control tower at the Miami Airport of the problem and got permission to circle at 2,000 feet over the nearby Everglades, a huge swampy region in Southern Florida, while the crew checked things out.

The pilot set the automatic flight controller ("automatic pilot") for that circling path and the crew began to investigate. One crew member looked through a peephole to check the landing-gear mechanism itself. Meanwhile, another crew member got a spare bulb in case the indicator bulb *was* burned out. During the next few minutes, someone either accidentally flipped a switch or very slightly jarred the pilot's control "stick." Whatever the cause, the automatic pilot control setting changed from holding the plane's altitude to a slow and steady descent.

The crew must have been so involved in trouble-shooting that no one heard the chime that sounds when the plane passes below an altitude of 1,750 feet. By the time they were certain that the landing gear was safely down and locked, they were dangerously close to

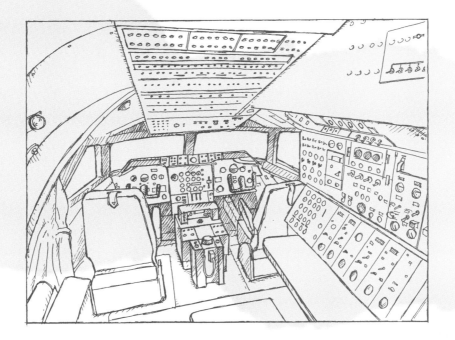

the ground. When the pilot turned sharply to head back to the airport for landing, a wingtip hit the swampy ground and broke off. The plane crashed, killing nearly 100 people.

The National Transportation Safety Board investigation of the accident determined that the "probable cause" of the crash of Flight 401 was the crew's inattention to instruments that would have warned them about the unexpected descent. Oddly, the accident probably would not have taken place in bad weather. Looking out the windows on that clear night, the crew could see the airport lights in the distance on each pass around the circle, while the dark swamp was nearly invisible. The crew's eyes told them that they were circling at 2,000 feet, as planned. Their altimeter, had they watched it, would have told them they were in danger.

Even though human error was the main cause of the tragedy, the NTSB report recommended several safety improvements to the aircraft itself. Those improvements would make it easier to check on the landing gear and to alert the crew to unexpected changes in altitude. After all, Murphy's Law tells us to expect people—even highly trained and well-prepared ones—to make mistakes. It is important to design our planes so that ordinary human error does not produce catastrophic results.

Flight 401 was the first wide-body plane to go down. So the findings of the NTSB were especially important—and not all were negative. The plane hit the ground so hard that no one would have been expected to survive. But the superior design of the passenger seats on the L-1011 saved more than 70 lives.

December 29, 1972, Everglades crash

Even the crew's attention to altimeters and a superior seat design did not save the lives of 257 people on board an Air New Zealand DC-10 sightseeing flight over Antarctica on November 28, 1979. The plane was approaching one of the trip's highlights, a close-up view of the active volcano Mount Erebus, when it smashed into the side of the mountain.

Again, the clear weather was a factor in the crash. This time the plane's crew was prepared for a white-out, an unusual situation that occurs over Antarctica on such days. When light reflects from the crystals of snow and passes through the frigid polar air, everything ahead looks white.

So the crew carefully watched the altimeter as their automatic pilot guided them along their usual path across the snowy terrain. Their instruments told them they were traveling at a low altitude, but high enough to safely clear the famous volcano, which—they thought—was just off to the side.

The crew and all aboard probably died without even having time to be surprised when they smashed into the mountain. The crew did not know that the airline had changed the automatic pilot's built-in flight path, which made it necessary to fly a bit higher past Mount Erebus. Someone had forgotten to tell them!

Chapter 4

Countdown to Disaster

Who could have imagined that children born around the time of the Wright brothers' first flight, in 1903, would be the parents of the first adventurers to travel in space and walk on the moon? Who could have predicted that the many miraculous machines that make space flight possible would soon be invented?

Today, although space travel is still special, it's no longer far-fetched. You may dream of being aboard the first spacecraft to rocket away from Earth, stop at a space station to pick up fuel and supplies, then set off on a multimillion-mile trip to Mars.

Along the way, you and your crewmates would surely talk about the people who traveled in space before you, including those who never reached their goals. In space travel, as in every other area of human technological success, there have been failures. In the most memorable tragedy of the U.S. space program, a catastrophic failure of part of the spacecraft ended seven lives.

Challenger crew: *l. to r.,* back row, Ellison S. Onizuka, Christa McAuliffe, Gregory B. Jarvis, Judith A. Resnik; front row, Michael J. Smith, Francis R. (Dick) Scobee, Ronald E. McNair.

Anyone old enough to remember the 25th launch of a U.S. Space Shuttle on January 28, 1986, will never forget the awful news. Seventy-three seconds after *Challenger* lifted off, an orange fireball suddenly erupted. Two solid rocket boosters, still burning their fuel, flew wildly in opposite directions. The main Shuttle vehicle (often called the orbiter) was nearly 10 miles (16 kilometers) above and no longer visible from the launch site as it broke into pieces and began its plunge into the sea.

All seven astronauts, including teacher-in-space Christa McAuliffe, died either in the explosion or when the crew cabin hit the water at more than 200 miles (320 kilometers) per hour. The entire country mourned. President Ronald Reagan postponed his annual State of the Union address, which had been scheduled for that night. He quickly appointed a presidential commission to study the tragedy and report on what they found. He knew that there were many lessons to be learned.

Space Shuttle Design

To understand why *Challenger* blew apart, you must understand the basic design of the U.S. Space Shuttle. Unlike the first space vehicles, which were designed to be used only once, the Shuttle was designed to be used over and over.

Building a one-use spacecraft is not as wasteful as it seems. Launching a satellite or space vehicle requires a lot of fuel. The more weight you launch and the higher you launch it, the more fuel you need. Sometimes you save money by dropping an empty fuel tank instead of carrying it into space. If the fuel tank carries the rocket above most of the atmosphere before it is dropped, it will burn up like a meteor on the way down.

Of course, some spacecraft—such as the Space Shuttle and others designed to carry people—have parts that must be recovered regardless of the expense. The biggest problem is reentry. When these spacecraft strike the atmosphere at great speed, they get extremely hot. To withstand the enormous heat of reentry, the early recoverable spacecraft were protected by a heat shield made of a special material on the side that would hit the atmosphere. When the material reached the hottest temperature that it could withstand, it flaked off. The flakes carried the heat away with them. By the time the spacecraft slowed down to the point that its parachutes could open, the heat shield was nearly gone.

After the heat took its toll on the space capsule and its heat shield, it was less expensive to build a new one than to repair the old one. They were recoverable, but not reusable. The Space Shuttle was designed to be different. Except for one major part, it is reusable.

The most important part of the Shuttle is the orbiter. It carries the cargo and crew into space and then returns to earth after the mission. It looks like an oversized airplane. To protect it from burning up on reentry, it is covered with reusable heat-resistant tiles. Unlike the material on older heat shields, these tiles can withstand extremely high temperatures and absorb enormous amounts of heat without flaking away.

On the launch pad, the orbiter is strapped onto a huge tank that holds liquid fuel. The fuel lasts until the orbiter is nearly into orbit. Then the empty tank, little more than a steel can, falls back to Earth and is not recovered.

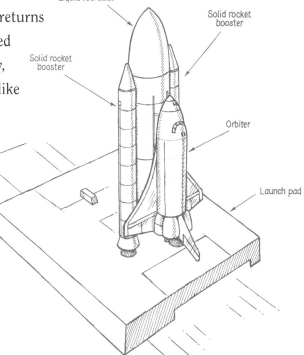

Liquid fuel tank

Solid rocket booster

Solid rocket booster

Orbiter

Launch pad

Also strapped to the tank are two solid rocket boosters (SRBs), each about one hundred feet long. The SRBs are like giant Roman candles in steel cases. Once ignited, they burn until their fuel is gone. The steel cases must be able to stand up to the high pressure of the gases produced in the burning. The gases escape at high speed through nozzles at the bottom of the SRBs and push the Shuttle upward. If you want to get an idea of how the SRBs work, blow up a balloon and pinch the opening closed, but do not tie it. When you release it, the air will escape rapidly from the opening, and the balloon will take off in the opposite direction.

The Space Shuttle's SRBs provide the extra force needed to lift the Shuttle through most of the atmosphere. Unlike the fuel tank, the SRBs have many valuable parts besides their fuel. This makes them worthwhile to recover.

The SRBs are too long to transport in one piece from the Morton-Thiokol Company in Utah, where they are made or refueled, to the Kennedy Space Center (KSC) in Florida, where the Shuttle is launched. Instead, the casings are loaded onto rail cars in four sections, each about 24 feet (7 meters) long and 14 feet (4 meters) in diameter. The sections are put together at KSC.

Making SRB sections that can be assembled without leaking requires skilled work and careful engineering. The engineers who designed the joints between SRB sections knew that hot gases escaping between sections could cause at least two problems. A leaky SRB would lose thrust or pushing power. Hot gases escaping in the direction of another part of the Shuttle could act like a blowtorch flame, melting or burning away parts that held the spacecraft together.

Warning Signs Ignored

When *Challenger* was launched on its final mission, some of those engineers were very worried about leaky SRB joints. Under the stresses of the flight through the atmosphere, the joints would have to flex. The engineers designed each joint with two large rubber "O-rings" and putty to close any gaps that might open during the launch. They included two O-rings for a reason that is common in spacecraft design: redundancy, the availability of a backup part in case the first one fails. When failure of a simple part could lead to loss of life or the spacecraft, engineers always try to include a back-up in their design.

After each Space Shuttle flight, the engineers examined the recovered SRBs for any sign of trouble. When they looked at the joints and O-rings, they found it. On most flights,

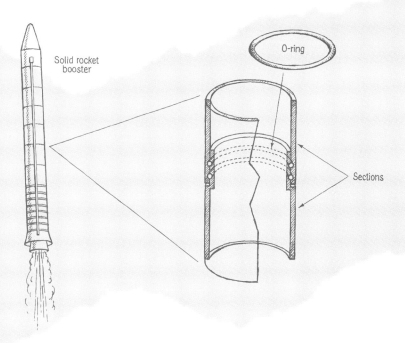

Solid rocket booster

O-ring

Sections

they saw soot, indicating that some hot gases had blown by some inner O-rings. The joints never leaked because the second O-ring held the seal. Because the "blow-by" happened so often, the second O-ring could no longer be considered redundant. Its designation was changed to "criticality 1," a term reserved for parts whose failure would surely lead to the loss of the mission, the spacecraft, and perhaps the astronauts' lives.

As the Space Shuttle project proceeded, its missions were scheduled closer together. The people in charge of the program wanted to show that the Shuttle could be a practical and economical way to take advantage of spaceflight. Meanwhile, a team of SRB engineers was designing a safer joint. Each flight gave them more information about the problems.

Because the rubber of the O-rings was stiffer at lower temperatures, the SRB engineers had a theory that the blow-by problem was worse on colder launch days. The theory seemed to be correct. For instance, the blow-by problem had been worst of all on the coldest launch day, when the outside temperature was 53°F. On January 27, when the KSC weather forecast called for a morning low below freezing and a launch-time temperature in the upper 30s, those engineers recommended that the flight be postponed.

That recommendation should have been enough to save *Challenger* from its doom, but it wasn't. The flight had been delayed several times already, and the Space Shuttle management team was concerned that another delay would push back other key missions scheduled later in the year. There was great pressure to launch the next morning as planned.

President Ronald Reagan was slated to discuss the Shuttle Program during his State of the Union Address that evening. Before the entire Congress of the United States and with the nation watching on television, the Shuttle's management hoped the President would celebrate Christa McAuliffe's greatest lesson in his most important speech of the year.

Instead of celebrating that night, the entire nation grieved. Political leaders planned an investigation into the *Challenger* tragedy.

What Went Wrong?

The investigation revealed a catastrophic failure. As the SRB engineers had feared, the cold weather stiffened the O-rings. A careful examination of a photograph taken less than a half-second after liftoff shows a puff of black smoke escaping from the bottom joint of the right-

Chapter 5

Fission with Melted Rods

Can you imagine living without electricity? Every year, people invent new electrical and electronic machines. Every year electrical and electronic technology spreads to more people in more countries around the world. Every year worldwide demand for electricity grows. Every year more or bigger electric power plants are needed to satisfy that demand.

For nearly 30 years following the end of World War II in 1945, the demand for electricity grew at an amazing rate. And it looked as if it would continue to grow at the same rate for decades to come. During this period, most electric power plants used steam to turn immense generators. The steam came from boiling water heated by burning fossil fuels (coal, oil, and natural gas) in huge furnaces. Some of the people who ran electric companies began to worry about getting enough fuel for their generators. Would we use up all the coal, oil, or natural gas? Would the countries with the greatest supplies of these fuels be able to control the world?

Meanwhile, the world had seen the great power released by the atomic bomb at the end of the war. In August 1945, two American atomic bombs of awesome power had devastated the Japanese cities of Hiroshima and Nagasaki. Could that power be harnessed to produce electricity? How wonderful it would be to turn the greatest technology of destruction into a force that could improve lives. Many engineers and scientists believed it could be done and set out to prove they could do it.

In 1958, the first commercial nuclear power plant, which used atomic power, went into operation at Shippingport, Pennsylvania, on the Beaver River about 20 miles (32 kilometers) west of Pittsburgh. Residents of Pittsburgh at that time remember the news reports: The power plant produced so much energy from so little fuel that electricity would someday be "too cheap to meter." They viewed themselves as pioneers.

Doubts and Fears

Still, many people feared the new technology. They remembered that the Hiroshima and Nagasaki bombs produced not only huge amounts of energy but also spread clouds of radioactivity. People exposed to the greatest radioactivity died in agony within days or weeks. Others developed cancers that killed them years later. Still others were no longer able to conceive children or risked having babies with terrible birth defects. Could electricity that nuclear power plants produced cause similar harm?

The experts—correctly—assured the public that no radioactivity would come through the wires to their home. The experts also assured them, again correctly, that the fuel in nuclear power plants could not explode like a bomb. Most experts also insisted that there was virtually no risk to public safety from the radioactive material in the power plant, even in the most severe accident they could imagine. Following Murphy's Law, they believed that they had anticipated every failure. They believed that a person was more likely to be harmed by a falling meteorite than by a nuclear power plant accident.

They may have been overconfident. Two major power plant accidents—one in 1979 at Three Mile Island (TMI), near Harrisburg, Pennsylvania, and one in 1986 at Chornobyl, near Prypyat, Ukraine (then part of the Soviet Union)—destroyed reactors and released radioactivity into the environment.

In the Three Mile Island accident, the amount of radioactivity released was small and there is no evidence of significant public harm from it. The Chornobyl accident was and continues to be a terrible human tragedy.

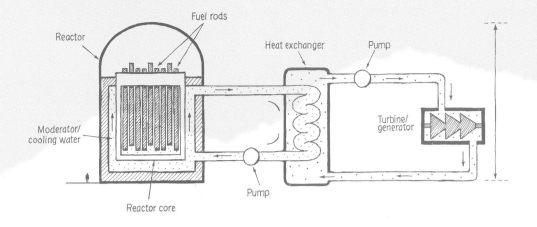

Fuel rods

Reactor

Heat exchanger

Pump

Moderator/
cooling water

Turbine/
generator

Reactor core

Pump

ing another nucleus and causing another fission. The most common moderators are water and graphite, a form of carbon used in "lead" pencils. Most commercial reactors use water. The water not only moderates the neutrons but also absorbs the great heat of the reaction. It is therefore called the cooling water, because it keeps the temperature of the reactor core under control. Despite its name, the cooling water becomes extremely hot. It either becomes superheated steam in a boiling water reactor or is kept from boiling by high pressure in a pressurized water reactor.

Pumps circulate this high-temperature water or steam to a heat exchanger, where the heat is used to boil water from a nearby lake or stream. That creates the steam that drives the generator. Since the water used as moderator becomes radioactive, it must be kept in a closed loop of plumbing. In the heat exchanger, only heat, not water, passes between the two loops of plumbing, one that contains the moderator and the other that contains the steam that drives the generator.

Among the fuel rods in the reactor core are a small number of control rods. These are made of a material that absorbs neutrons. Gravity and strong springs hold the control rods in place. That prevents a nuclear chain reaction from starting, even with the moderator present. The reactor can produce power only when the control rods are forcibly withdrawn against the springs.

A nuclear explosion is not possible in such reactors. First, the control rods prevent a runaway chain reaction. Second, long before the nuclear fuel could explode, the moderator would be lost through ruptured pipes (in the case of water-moderated reactors) or combustion (in the case of graphite-moderated reactors). Finally, the fuel itself is not sufficiently enriched to explode.

Still, the fission products and extreme heat in the reactor are major causes for concern. Even when the reactor is not producing power, the core must be cooled. Otherwise the heat from the radioactivity of the fission products would raise the temperature of the fuel rods above their melting point. If the heat melted the steel containment vessel of the core, this meltdown could dangerously pollute the ground and threaten water supplies.

With so much heat and high pressure present, nuclear power plant designers must also worry about a nonnuclear explosion, which could blast fission products into the atmosphere. For that reason, most countries require a reinforced concrete containment building around all commercial nuclear reactors.

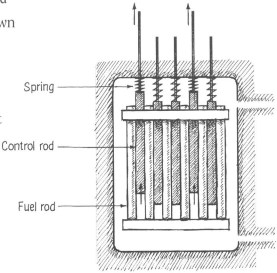

Concern for Public Safety

Since the beginning of nuclear power production in the United States, critics have complained about the industry's safety standards. Commercial reactor development began with the encouragement of the Atomic Energy Commission (AEC), a government agency with two jobs. One was to encourage companies to develop peaceful uses of nuclear energy. The other was to assure public safety when nuclear energy is used.

Critics complained that the AEC could not do both jobs. It is impossible to be both a watchdog and a cheerleader at the same time, they said. In the mid-1970s, the AEC was dissolved, and the Nuclear Regulatory Commission (NRC) was created as a watchdog in its place. Still, critics claimed that the NRC was too tightly connected with the industry.

That was far from the only problem facing nuclear power. Demand for electricity was not increasing at the predicted rate. The industry also had to deal with environmental concerns, such as what to do with nuclear waste. Both slow growth and increased environmental awareness delayed projects for years. These delays, more than any other factor, greatly increased the cost of building a new reactor. The leaders of the electric power industry realized that nuclear-produced electricity would never be too cheap to meter. Instead, they now feared that it would be too expensive to sell.

Thus, the outlook of the nuclear industry in the late 1970s had become bleak. Then, to make things worse, came TMI.

Accident at TMI

About 11 miles (18 kilometers) downstream from Harrisburg, Pennsylvania, on the Susquehanna River is Three Mile Island (TMI). There, in the early 1970s, the Babcock & Wilcox (B&W) Corporation built two pressurized water nuclear reactors to be the heart of a major new electrical generating facility for Metropolitan Edison and its parent company, the General Public Utilities (GPU) Corporation.

B&W was one of four U.S. companies building and selling nuclear reactors for the electric power industry and one of three building pressurized water reactors. Besides the TMI project, B&W built similar reactors at many sites, including the Davis-Besse plant on the shore of Lake Erie just east of Toledo, Ohio. The B&W design met all the standards set by the NRC.

But in September 1977 an incident at Davis-Besse almost caused the loss of the plant. Two problems occurred. The first, a bad indicator on the control panel, went unnoticed and was harmless until the second problem occurred: a stuck valve. Fortunately, a highly trained shift supervisor was on duty. Even more fortunately was that the plant had been operating at low power.

A B&W engineer investigating the Davis-Besse incident wrote a report that clearly explained what had gone wrong. It might have made a difference at TMI, but the report somehow got stuck in routine company channels. Almost no one read the engineer's warning and advice in time.

An NRC investigator was also concerned, but his supervisors paid no attention. Finally, he decided to risk his job and speak personally to two NRC commissioners. They took him seriously, and on March 21, 1979, they ordered an investigation.

That investigation came too late. One week later, at 4:00 A.M. on the morning of March 28, 1979, a pressure relief valve stuck open in the core cooling loop at TMI unit number 2. The plant was operating at a higher power level than Davis-Besse had been, and no one realized the valve was open until severe damage had been done. It was several days before public safety was ensured, and the consequences of the incident continue until this day.

The problem began at a time when routine maintenance work had stopped the flow of feedwater from the river to the steam generators. The plant's safety system automatically went to work, dropping control rods into the core and switching on emergency feedwater pumps. Two valves had accidentally been left closed, so no emergency water could flow through the heat exchanger. Thus, the cooling water could not get rid of the heat it was absorbing from the decaying fission products in the reactor core. Pressure built up in the cooling loop, until a pressure relief valve opened.

Alarms alerted the reactor operators to the open pressure relief valve. Quickly, they realized the cause of the excess heat and pressure and opened the valves to start the flow of emergency feedwater. The pressure in the cooling water loop quickly returned to a safe level. An operator pushed a button to close the pressure relief valve. An indicator light on the panel turned on when he did that, but the valve did not close. Stuck open, it let precious cooling water escape. As the dropping water level uncovered more and more of the reactor core, a catastrophic meltdown began.

Alarms sounded and warning lights flashed all over the control room. It was a major emergency. Because workers thought the cooling water pressure relief valve was closed, they looked for other causes first. One temperature gauge would have pinpointed the prob-

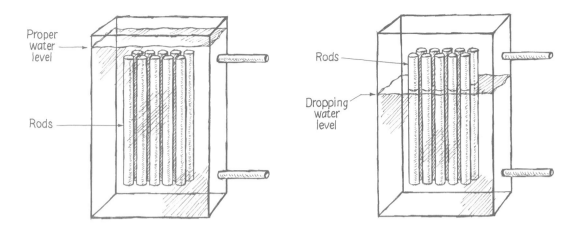

Proper water level

Rods

Rods

Dropping water level

lem valve, but in the confusion, an operator read the wrong one.

It was 16 hours before the loss of cooling water was stopped, and the core, 12 feet (3.7 meters) high, was once again submerged. By then, the upper two thirds of the core had been destroyed. So much cooling water had escaped through the open valve that the radioactive waste storage tanks overflowed and released some radioactivity into the atmosphere.

At that point, no one knew the extent of damage to the core. It seemed that a meltdown had been narrowly averted and the reactor would eventually be restarted. On March 29, a spokesman for GPU declared the emergency over and said, "There was nothing catastrophic or unplanned for."

By the evening of the next day, he had to eat his words. The most terrifying period of the incident at TMI had just begun.

In all the years of reactor safety studies, no one had anticipated that melted metal cladding of fuel rods can react chemically with water to produce hydrogen gas. By late in the day on March 30, it was clear that was happening. A bubble of hydrogen was growing inside the core. The public feared that the gas would ignite and explode, but that was unlikely since it wasn't mixing with air.

The engineers feared something worse. As the bubble grew, more and more of the core was no longer in contact with cooling water. The meltdown could resume and this time melt through the steel containment vessel. If melted fuel went into the soil, the natural flow of rainwater could disastrously pollute the environment with fission products.

Pennsylvania officials hastily drew up evacuation plans. Governor Richard Thornburgh urged pregnant women and preschool children within 5 miles (about 9 kilometers) of TMI to leave the area. Many other people—about 100,000 altogether—were concerned enough to leave their homes.

Fortunately, the bubble problem was solved and the crisis passed quickly. It took a few weeks after that for the reactor to cool enough to be considered stable. Radioactivity measurements indicated that no one outside the immediate area of the reactor complex had been exposed to more than minor amounts of excess radiation.

Those measurements did not stop people from believing that they had suffered physical harm from the incident. Some people still believe that there were an unusually large number of birth defects, stillbirths, miscarriages, and cancers in the area after the TMI incident. No scientific evidence supports their claim, but they remain convinced. After all, wasn't it scientists who told them how safe nuclear power could be?

After well over a decade of work and billions of dollars of clean-up costs, the debate continues over what TMI says about nuclear power plant safety. Since the only serious damage from the catastrophic events at TMI were to the plant itself, some people declare that nuclear power plants protect the public and the environment even in the worst possible accident. Others argue that we should view TMI as a warning that nuclear technology is unavoidably more complicated than people can handle, even though we have learned and applied many important safety lessons from it.

Analysis of the TMI accident continues to produce surprises. In late 1993, scientists reported on studies of samples recovered from the reactor vessel during the clean-up. They found that the molten core had hardened into a brittle crust at the bottom of the containment vessel. This crust proved to be an unplanned safety feature. It was full of cracks that permitted water to flow through, cooling the containment vessel just enough to save it.

Tragedy at Chornobyl

The nuclear reactors at the Chornobyl power complex were built according to a design that relies on graphite as the moderator. In such a design the cooling water is more of an absorber of neutrons than a moderator. It flows through the reactor core in pipes rather than being contained in a pressurized vessel with the fuel and control rods.

Unlike reactors in which the water serves as both moderator and absorber, graphite-moderated reactors would continue their chain reaction in a loss-of-coolant accident. In fact, without an absorber, more neutrons would be available to continue the chain reaction.

After a loss of cooling water, the power would increase rapidly until the graphite would ignite in a fiery non-nuclear explosion.

The Chornobyl accident began not long after midnight on April 25, 1986, when reactor operators performed an ill-conceived test of a safety system. A Soviet nuclear scientist said it was "like airline pilots experimenting with the engines in flight."

The operators reduced the flow of cooling water and turned off a generator that powered some of the cooling water pumps. Less cooling water now had to absorb the same amount of heat as it passed through the core. Suddenly it began to boil. The reactor surged out of control. The graphite moderator flashed into flames. Two explosions tore open the plant's side and roof and shattered the core's lid, which weighed a thousand tons.

Workers hose down a truck contaminated with fallout from Chornobyl.

On May 6, by the time the fires were brought under control 31 people, mostly fire fighters, were dead or dying of radiation poisoning. In addition, 4 percent of the fission products from the reactor core had been blasted into the atmosphere—more radioactive material than was released by both U.S. atomic bombs dropped on Japan at the end of World War II.

In comparison to the TMI accident, Chornobyl released three million times as much radioactivity. Even worse, the radioactive fallout spread throughout the earth's northern hemisphere.

So much fell on the large city of Kiev, 80 miles (about 130 kilometers) to the south of Chornobyl, that it has caused cancers and birth defects ever since. People in other northern European countries may also be suffering the same problems, but scientists have not been able to link their problems directly to Chornobyl.

What Now?

Beyond the human toll, the most significant "fallout" of these two catastrophic accidents is their effects on the worldwide nuclear power industry. Although concerns about diminishing fossil fuels continue to drive some countries to develop nuclear power programs, most countries have stopped building or designing new nuclear plants.

In the United States, nuclear safety regulations have become stricter and more

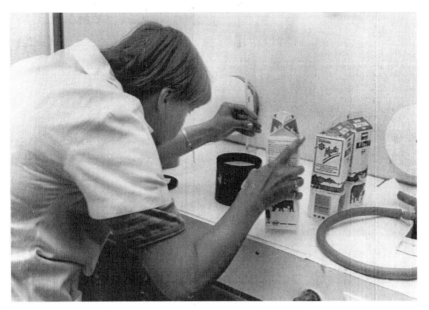

A scientist tests milk for radiation levels.

detailed, and concerns about nuclear waste disposal have not been resolved. Still, the most significant changes for nuclear power are economic. As people conserve energy and as the economy grows more slowly than in earlier decades, the demand for new power plants is much smaller than estimated 20 years ago. The supply of fossil fuels is high and the prices are low.

From the United States' point of view, the world political situation is less threatening. Fewer people worry that our supply of imported oil will be threatened. Most people are willing to accept the environmental hazards of fossil-fuel-burning electric power plants. As a result of these political and economic conditions, no new nuclear plants have been started in the U.S. in more than a decade.

Still, sometime in your lifetime, the question of nuclear power is likely to arise again. The designs will be safer, the plans for waste disposal will be better, and the concerns about other sources of electric power will grow.

Both sides will argue that we have learned the lessons of TMI and Chornobyl. One side will say that the lessons teach us that nuclear power plant technology will always be too risky to try. The other side will say that the we have learned the lessons of failure and that we can succeed in spite of the risks.

Coming to the right decision then will be no easier than it is now, nor will it be any less important. TMI and Chornobyl are two spectacular failures from which we will be learning for a long time.

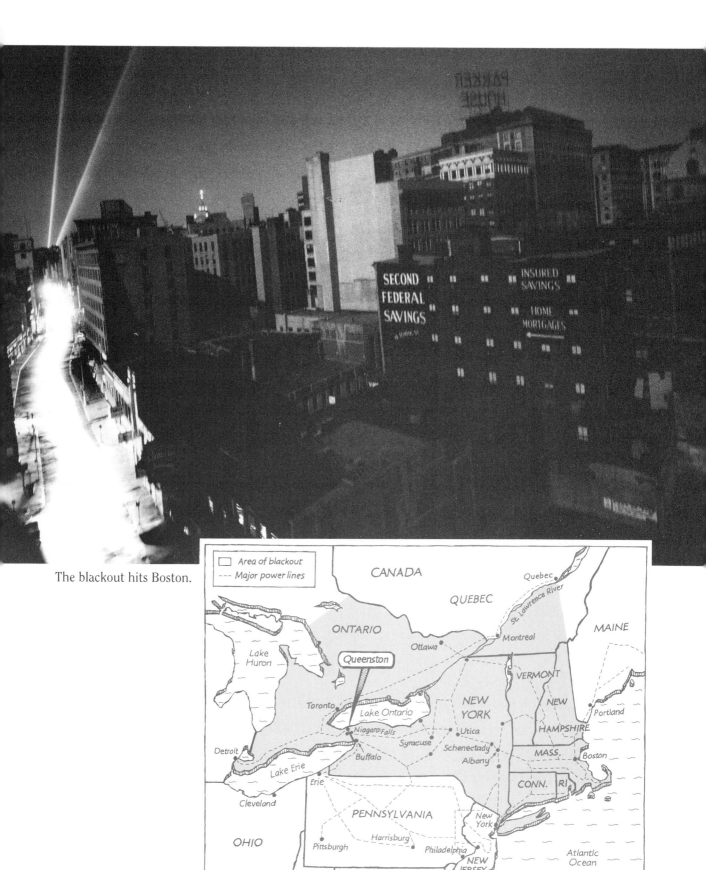

The blackout hits Boston.

Area of blackout
Major power lines

CANADA

QUEBEC

Quebec

St. Lawrence River

ONTARIO

MAINE

Ottawa

Montreal

Queenston

VERMONT

NEW
HAMPSHIRE

Portland

Lake
Huron

Toronto

Lake Ontario

NEW
YORK

Niagara Falls

Utica

Syracuse

Schenectady

Detroit

Buffalo

Albany

MASS.

Boston

Lake Erie

Erie

CONN.

RI

Cleveland

PENNSYLVANIA

New
York

OHIO

Pittsburgh

Harrisburg

Philadelphia

NEW
JERSEY

Atlantic
Ocean

Chapter 6

Who Turned Out the Lights?

At 5:15 P.M. on November 9, 1965, the Tuesday evening rush hour was near its peak in New York City. Bright city lights were taking over from the setting sun as 800,000 people crowded into subways and elevated trains. Thousands of others were in elevators, heading toward the street from their offices in Manhattan's skyscrapers, while thousands more stayed behind to work a little late.

The streets below were filled with the honking of countless horns as drivers, impatient with each other and with red lights, beeped at snarled traffic. In hospitals, doctors and nurses worked together to help new mothers give birth, to perform delicate surgery, and to care for patients attached to life-sustaining machinery. In the sky above the city, airplanes circled La Guardia and Kennedy airports. In the heavy air traffic and the fading evening light, pilots were relying on radio messages from controllers and runway lights to guide them safely to a landing. As they went about their business, few took the time to think about what would happen to them if the city suddenly lost all electric power.

Meanwhile, in Conway, New Hampshire, 11-year-old Jay Hounsell was ambling along, enjoying his thoughts and the crisp New England autumn air. He picked up a stick and swung it back and forth. He passed a telephone pole and took a whack at it.

Similar scenes were taking place in large and small cities across the Northeastern United States and neighboring Canada: Boston, Massachusetts; Hartford, Connecticut; Providence, Rhode Island; Montpelier, Vermont; Albany, Buffalo, Rochester, and Syracuse, New York; Erie, Pennsylvania; Toronto, Queenston, and Niagara Falls, Ontario. It was an ordinary day, but it would soon become an unforgettable one. In all those places, almost all at once, the power was about to go out.

In the next minute, a protective relay "tripped" in order to prevent an electrical over-load at generating station number 2 of the Sir Adam Beck electric power complex near Queenston, a small city in Ontario, Canada, along the Niagara River a few miles upstream from the famous falls. That simple action of a simple device set off a chain of events that, within 12 minutes, shut off electric power to more than 30 million people over an area of 80,000 square miles (210,000 square kilometers).

Jay Hounsell was sure it was all his fault. Just as his stick made contact with that

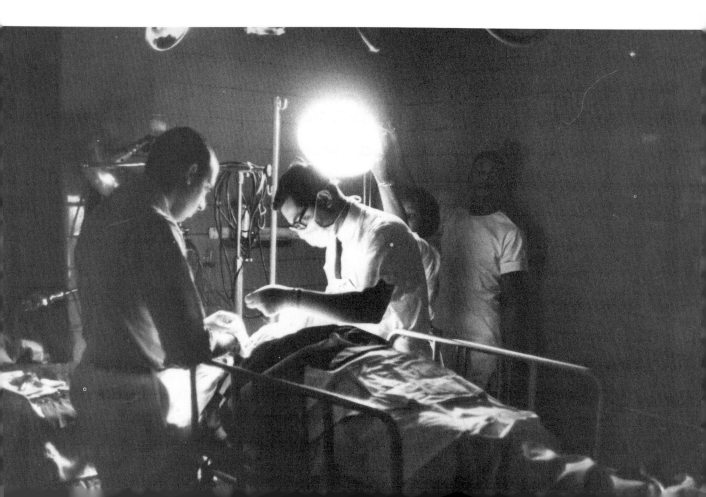

pole, the event that would soon be called "The Great Northeast Blackout" swept through Conway. He went home and confessed to his mother that his harmless bit of mischief had caused the whole thing!

Grids and Interties

In 1965, the demand for electric power in the United States was growing at about 7% per year. In some regions of the country, the growth rate was a lot larger. To keep up with the demand, electric utilities companies built more and bigger power plants.

Among the most important concerns to an electric company is the ability to keep up with its peak load, the maximum rate of energy use by its customers. Because of climate, the economy, and other available sources of energy in its service area, each electric company has a different peak-load profile: different sizes, different times of day, different seasons of the year.

To meet that peak load, and to have some reserve capacity for times that a power plant is out of service for maintenance or repairs, each electric company takes a different approach. Some build additional power stations; other choose to buy power from another utility that is not using its full capacity at the time. For one company to buy or sell power to another, the two must build a transmission line to connect them.

At first, electric utilities formed regional networks for exchanging power. In case of trouble on one utility's lines, transmission lines include electrically controlled switches, called relays, that can disconnect the utility from the network. Relays can be automatically or manually controlled.

By 1965, these regional networks began to interconnect with one another at points called interties. A national network, which actually crossed the U.S.-Canadian border, had begun to take shape. About 90% of the U.S. population was served by electric companies on that grid.

Most experts agreed that a full national network would save money, but some worried that an accidental or deliberate incident in Conway, New Hampshire, could knock out power in San Francisco, California, and everywhere in between. They asked, Could a system be built that would always keep power failures from spreading?

Concerns like that were in the air when the lights went out all over the Northeast. Even after the cause of the blackout was fully understood, the answers to those questions were still in dispute.

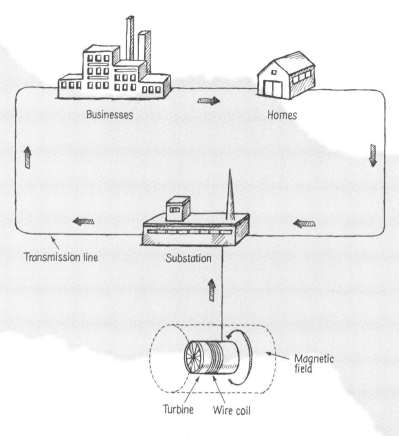

Businesses

Homes

Transmission line

Substation

Magnetic field

Turbine   Wire coil

Generator

Of Generators, Turbines, and Relays

Electric power systems have many large, expensive pieces of equipment that carry huge amounts of electrical energy. The most important piece of equipment is the generator. A generator produces electricity by turning a huge cylinder called a turbine in a magnetic field. That motion causes an electric current to flow in wires wrapped around the turbine. The turbine is connected to transmission lines, which send the electricity to substations. From the substations the electricity is distributed to homes and businesses.

In the United States, Canada, and many other countries, commercial electric power generators produce alternating electric current that cycles from one direction of flow to the other and back again precisely sixty times every second. (In other parts of the world the rate is precisely fifty cycles per second.) To maintain this precision, the turbine speed must remain constant. To maintain constant turbine speed, the power put into the turbine must precisely match the power it puts out.

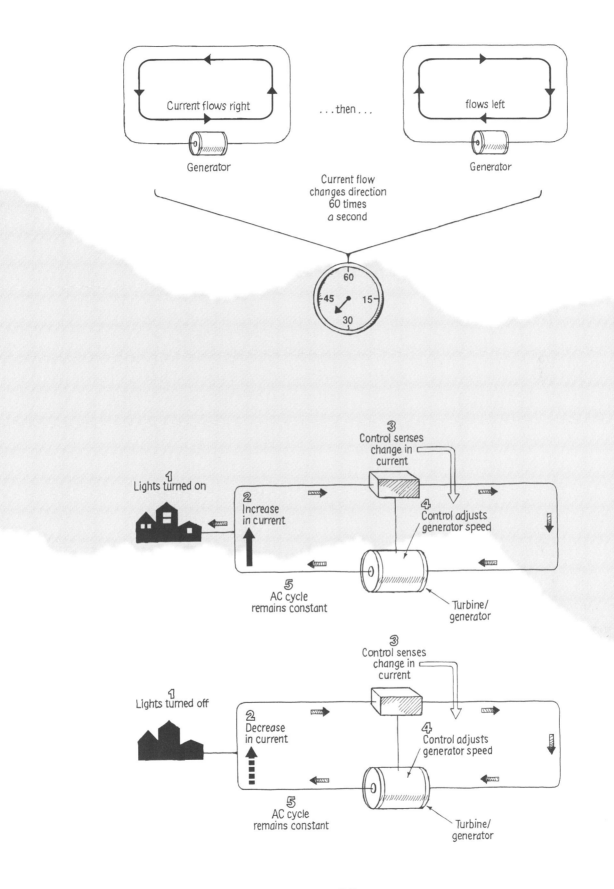

Current flows right

...then...

flows left

Generator

Generator

Current flow
changes direction
60 times
a second

60

45   15

30

3
Control senses
change in
current

1
Lights turned on

2
Increase
in current

4
Control adjusts
generator speed

5
AC cycle
remains constant

Turbine/
generator

3
Control senses
change in
current

1
Lights turned off

2
Decrease
in current

4
Control adjusts
generator speed

5
AC cycle
remains constant

Turbine/
generator

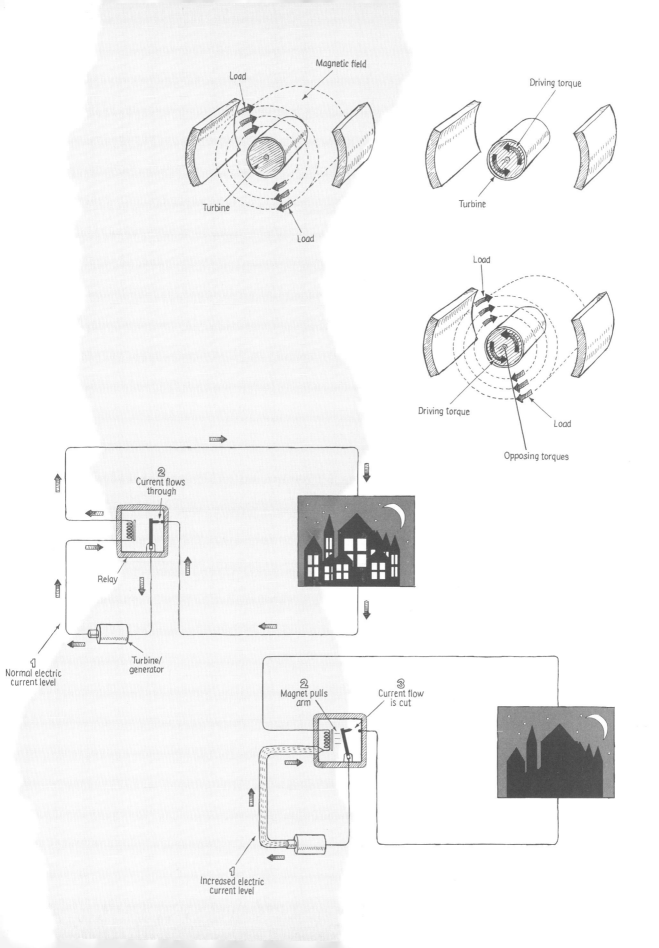

Load

Magnetic field

Driving torque

Turbine

Turbine

Load

Load

Load

Driving torque

Opposing torques

2
Current flows
through

Relay

Turbine/
generator

1
Normal electric
current level

2
Magnet pulls
arm

3
Current flow
is cut

1
Increased electric
current level

Commercial electric generators must be designed with control systems that maintain that precision. Every time someone switches a light bulb on or off, every time a refrigerator motor starts or stops, every time a conveyer belt in a factory slows down or speeds up, the amount of electrical current drawn from the generator changes. As the turbine turns, it experiences two opposing rotational forces, or torques. The control system keeps these torques in balance.

One torque, the load, tends to slow the turbine; the other, the driving torque, tends to speed it up. Most of the load is due to the electromagnetic force between the current in the turbine and the surrounding magnetic field. A smaller amount is due to mechanical effects such as friction. In fossil fuel and nuclear plants, the driving torque comes from steam produced by the heat of the burning fuel or the nuclear reaction. In hydroelectric plants, it is produced by falling water.

When the current in the turbine increases, the load increases. An automatic control mechanism senses the turbine slowing ever so slightly and calls for more steam or more water flow. When the current decreases, the load decreases and the driving force tends to turn the generator too fast. Again, the control mechanism senses the change in speed, and this time calls for less steam or water flow.

If the generator cannot change speed quickly enough, safety devices in the control system, usually relays, go into action. They disconnect the generator and shut it down. This protects the generator and the devices connected to it from damage due to overheating or too much mechanical stress.

The power transmission system uses relays for protection against electrical overloads in many places. When the current in a wire or device becomes too high, a protective relay trips, and the current stops. (The relay also trips if it loses power. In other words, it is "fail-safe," as a good protective device should be.)

A relay can be set to trip at whatever current the circuit designer chooses. The relay that set off the Great Northeast Blackout was set to trip at too low a current.

What a Trip!

The Sir Adam Beck generating station number 2 near Queenston, Ontario, turned some of the power of the fast-flowing Niagara River into electricity for millions of people in Ontario and Quebec provinces. Just before the blackout, it was generating nearly its full capacity of

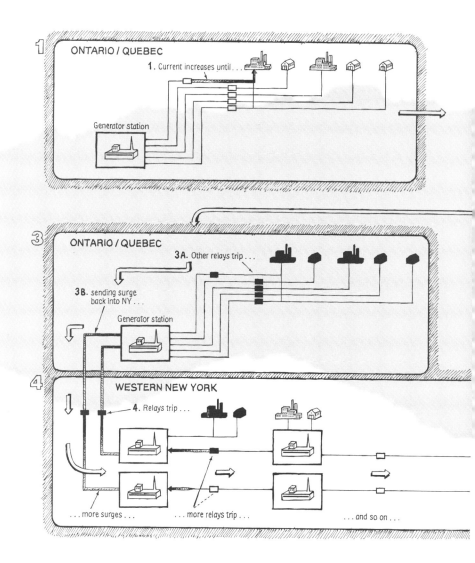

one million kilowatts—enough to serve hundreds of thousands of households. In addition, the Beck station was drawing an additional half-million kilowatts from two power companies in western New York State. The Beck station then sent its 1.5 million kilowatts eastward on five huge transmission lines.

Each of the transmission lines was protected by a relay about the size of a shoe box. The trip-points of those relays were supposed to be reset periodically as the lines were upgraded. Unfortunately, one of the relays was missed, and on November 9, 1965, it still guarded against power levels set in 1963. It was only a matter of time before a short surge of power would trip the relay.

When the first relay tripped, the full 1.5 million kilowatts was suddenly divided among the remaining four transmission lines. That was more than they could safely carry, so their relays quickly tripped, plunging Toronto into darkness.

by areas that drew power from New Jersey, went dark, and with it went the rest of the Northeast. Con Ed suffered more damage than any other company; it was nearly 10 hours before any of the City's power was restored.

In 1990, as the 25th anniversary of the Great Northeast Blackout approached, electric power engineers asked, "Can it happen again?" Their answer was yes. Not only can it happen again, but it will happen again, unless we obey Murphy's Law for electric power networks! With power plants in the United States and Canada more connected and interlocking than in the 1960s, and with the average person far more dependent on electricity, a repeat of the "cascading blackout" would be far more devastating.

Potholes on the Information Superhighway

The Great Northeast Blackout has lessons that go far beyond electric power generation. The United States and Canada—and indeed the entire world—are becoming more and more dependent on interconnections and networks. Our lives are enriched by our ability to get information of all kinds—printed words, sounds, images, and computer files—quickly and accurately. Yet at the same time, we are becoming more dependent on our networked technology: our phones, Faxes, cable televisions, and computers.

Experts predict that by the third decade of the 21st century, nearly all American households, businesses, schools, hospitals, and other institutions will be connected by thin strands of glass called fiberoptic cables to the "Information Superhighway." The Information Superhighway will be a giant network designed to carry information of all kinds: 500 television channels, telephone conversations, video images and programs, and computer information, to name just a few.

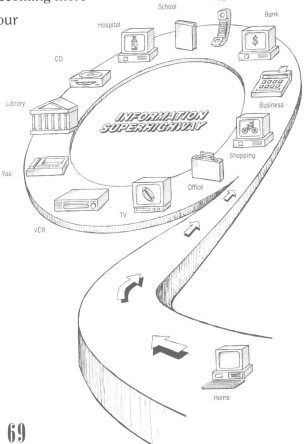

Telephones, televisions, VCRs, compact disc players, and home computers will blend together into information and telecommunication machines. You'll be able to do your shopping, carry out your bank business, meet people, and do most of your office work from the comfort of your home. Neighborhoods may be global, offices may be virtual. Libraries will give you access to thousands of times as much knowledge as ever before, in words, diagrams, databases, and images of all kinds.

Looking back to the mid-19th century, you can see dramatic changes in where and how people lived as new technologies became available. The railroads, the telegraph, the telephone, electrification, radio, television, the interstate highway system, and computers have changed the pattern of life, in many parts of the world.

Each new technological advance produced greater changes than the one that came before it. The Information Superhighway promises the most dramatic changes of all.

Each new technology has also brought with it a new set of failures—some catastrophic—to learn from. The Great Northeast Blackout is a warning to watch out for potholes on the Information Superhighway.

There have already been a few hints about what those potholes might be. In the summer of 1991, telephone customers in four major United States metropolitan areas—Washington, D.C., San Francisco and Los Angeles, California, and Pittsburgh, Pennsylvania—suddenly and mysteriously lost service, sometimes for as long as eight hours. Engineers eventually traced the problem to a change in the computer program—the software—that controlled the switching and connection of local phone calls. A "bug" caused problems only when the calling load was heavy. Then, like the Great Northeast Blackout, it caused a catastrophic cascade of disconnections and blockages. No one in the affected areas could get a dial tone.

Since the traffic on the Information Superhighway will be guided and controlled by software, human errors and mechanical or electrical failures are bound to cause unanticipated problems from time to time. Engineers know that, so they are trying to design systems in which the consequences of failure will be small and controllable. They are also looking for ways to improve the writing and testing of new software so your ride on the Information Superhighway of the future will be smooth and pothole free.

Respecting the Power of Failure

You have seen example after example of what Murphy's Law really means: *If you want things to go right, pay attention to everything that can go wrong.* It is far easier to understand Murphy's Law than it is to follow it. How do engineers anticipate everything that can go wrong? It's a matter of attitude, they say. *A good engineer respects the power of failure.* Some of the best places to look at this are in natural disasters, such as earthquakes, hurricanes, and floods. These put incredible strain on buildings and other structures.

When a large earthquake strikes California, it is big news across the United States. On October 17, 1989, millions of people were watching pregame television coverage of the World Series from San Francisco when a major earthquake (measured at 6.9 on the Richter scale) struck. The stadium shook and cracked in places, but the structure withstood the tremor and there were no serious physical injuries to people there.

Elsewhere in the San Francisco Bay Area, 60 people died. The most deaths occurred under collapsed highway overpasses, on partially collapsed bridges, and in fires set off by broken natural gas lines.

In the early morning hours of January 17, 1994, a quake of similar strength (6.6 on the Richter scale) struck just north of Los Angeles. More than 30 people died, some in highway collapses. The largest number of deaths occurred in the collapse of a single apartment building which, unfortunately, was built directly above a previously unknown earthquake fault line.

In both of those earthquakes, the good news was that most buildings (including huge skyscrapers), overpasses, and bridges in the areas survived intact. The designers of those structures surely took pride in the fact that their artifacts had survived, but they and other engineers paid more attention to the bad news, the artifacts that failed.

They asked themselves many questions. Had the collapsed structures been designed

A San Francisco roadway collapses.

Mexico City

Iran

to withstand an earthquake of that strength? If so, were they built according to the design? If so, why didn't they live up to expectations? Do the collapses suggest changes to be made in building codes and in earthquake engineering practice? People who ask such questions respect the power of failure.

How powerful can failure of our structures be? A 1993 earthquake in Iran of similar intensity killed 10,000. In 1988 another similar earthquake killed over 60,000 people in Armenia. And in 1985, a pair of more powerful earthquakes (7.8 and 7.5 on the Richter scale) in Mexico City on consecutive days collapsed 250 buildings, killed 7,000 people, and left tens of thousands homeless.

In those deadly quakes, most of the buildings that failed had not been designed to withstand such stresses. The problem was not poor engineering but poverty. There was not enough money to design and build earthquake-resistant homes and other structures. To have homes, schools, and hospitals, the people gambled that a powerful earthquake would not strike nearby.

One of the most dramatic and deadly failures of a single structure was the collapse of the dam that created Lake Conemaugh in the Allegheny Mountains of Pennsylvania, 1 mile (1.6 kilometers) above and 9 miles (15 kilometers) to the east of the steel-making center of Johnstown. (By boat along the winding South Fork Creek and Little Conemaugh River, it was 15 miles [24 kilometers].)

On May 31, 1889, heavy rains filled the lake over the top of the dam, a wedge of earth and stones that was 72 feet (22 meters) high. The overflowing water eroded the structure and its supports. Suddenly, the dam could no longer hold back the weight of the water behind it.

Observers at the dam said that the massive structure moved before the water rushed over it and tore it apart. That unleashed a torrent. For more than 30 minutes, as much water as flows over Niagara Falls rushed into the narrow mountain valley. It surged downward, washing out small villages and bridges, tossing railroad trains and locomotives like toys.

At the bottom of the valley in Johnstown, the furious water rose to a depth of 23 feet (7 meters) and damaged or destroyed most of the homes, buildings, and factories in the city. Of the roughly 30,000 people living in the valley, more than 2,200 were killed.

Unlike the deadly earthquakes described earlier, it was great wealth, not poverty, that set the stage for tragedy in Johnstown. Wealthy industrialists from Pittsburgh had purchased an abandoned dam on South Fork Creek and rebuilt it to create Conemaugh Lake and develop a summer resort, the South Fork Fishing and Hunting Club, along its shores.

The original dam had a set of pipes that could be opened to drain some of the water from the lake to lower the water when needed. Those pipes had been damaged, and the dam was rebuilt without them. That left it with a permanent sag on top, 4 feet (1.2 meters) lower in its center than at its ends.

To prevent water from flowing over the top and eroding away the earthen structure, a spillway—a 72-foot-wide by 12-foot-deep (3.6-meter-deep) notch through which the water would flow—was cut into the rock at one end of the dam. With the sag, that meant the lake was usually 8 feet (2.4 meters) below the top of the dam in its center. In times of heavy rain, the water ran deeper in the spillway and came closer to overflowing the dam.

To create good fishing, the artificial lake behind the dam was stocked with trout and bass brought in from nearby natural lakes and streams. Unfortunately, the fish would go over the spillway. So the club members had the spillway covered with wire mesh. In heavy rain, leaves, branches, and other debris would partly block the spillway and raise the water a bit more behind the dam.

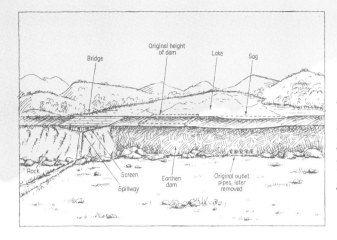

The diagram is not to exact scale because the sag would actually be too far from the bridge to be seen from this angle.

As if that weren't enough, the road along the top of the dam was too narrow. To widen it, they shaved off the top of the wedge until there was enough space for two carriages to pass each other. When that was done, the normal water level was within 4 feet (1.2 meters) of the low point in the dam's center.

Thus, Lake Conemaugh was a tragedy waiting to happen. When unusually heavy spring rains hit the mountains on that day in 1889, the lake disappeared, along with more than 2,200 lives. Suddenly, the South Fork Fishing and Hunting Club was an oddly placed cluster of luxurious cottages and buildings far above a small mountain creek, a monument to what can happen when people fail to respect the great power of failure.

Index

Photo Credits

Other Books You Might Enjoy

If you would like to know more about failures, how engineers learn from them, and how people deal with them, here are a few books that the author highly recommends.

Books for Young Readers

—*Living in a Risky World* by Laurence Pringle, published by William Morrow in 1989. Life is full of risks. This book describes how people and societies evaluate and come to terms with the risks of modern technology.

— *Nuclear Energy: Troubled Past, Uncertain Future* also by Laurence Pringle, published by Macmillan in 1989. This book gives a balanced view of the history of the nuclear power industry, describing not only its problems but also its potential benefits.

Books on Engineering, Failures, and Disasters for Adult Readers

— *To Engineer is Human: The Role of Failure in Successful Design* by Henry Petroski, published in hard cover by St. Martin's Press in 1985 and in slightly different form in paperback by Vintage Books in 1992. A lecture by Petroski inspired the author think about writing a book for young people on catastrophic failures. Now that you have read *Catastrophe!*, you may be able to understand and enjoy much of Petroski's book even though it is written for adults.

— The Design of Everyday Things by Donald A. Norman, originally called *The Psychology of Everyday Things*. This entertaining and informative book was published in hard cover by Basic Books in 1988, then slightly modified as a paperback and published by Doubleday in 1990. Reading *Catastrophe!* may enable you to understand and appreciate much of this adult book.

— *The Pessimist's Guide to History* by Stuart Flexner and Doris Flexner, published in paperback by Avon Books in 1992. This is an often humorous, chronological listing of catastrophic and disastrous events from the Big Bang to the present day. Even though it is written for adults, you might enjoy scanning it for events that might be included in a larger version of this book.

Books for Adults on Some of the Catastrophes in This Book

— *The Warning: Accident at Three Mile Island* by Mike Gray and Ira Rosen, published in hard cover by Norton and in paperback by Contemporary Books in 1982. The authors are investigative reporters, and this book tells the story of the TMI accident and its background events like a well-told mystery.

— *The Johnstown Flood* by David G. McCullough, published in hard cover by Simon and Schuster in 1968. Historian McCullough vividly describes the events leading up to the flood, the design and catastrophic failure of the dam, the passage of the huge mass of water through the mountains and into the valley, and the flood's consequences and aftermath.

— *Challenger: The Final Voyage* by Richard S. Lewis, published in hard cover by Columbia University Press in 1988. This is a detailed description of the tragic final flight of the Challenger, the findings of the investigation into the event, and the impact of those findings on future Shuttle missions. Despite its heavy dose of science and engineering, this book is very readable because of its many photographs and diagrams with excellent captions.